CGP

Speedy Workouts for every week of Year 6!

This CGP book is bursting with fantastic 10-Minute Workouts
to improve Spelling and Vocabulary week by week in Year 6.

Each Workout includes Spelling practice matched to the National
Curriculum, along with questions to expand pupils' Vocabulary and help
them learn how to deal with unfamiliar words — plus a fun puzzle too!

We've even included a handy chart to track progress over the
whole year, a checklist of tricky words and cut-out answers.

Published by CGP
ISBN: 978 1 78908 298 2

Editors: Eleanor Claringbold, Emma Crighton,
Becca Lakin, Harry Millican and James Summersgill

With thanks to Juliette Green and
Gabrielle Richardson for the proofreading.

With thanks to Emily Smith for the copyright research.

Contents pages and page 74 contain public sector
information licensed under the Open Government
Licence v3.0. http://www.nationalarchives.gov.
uk/doc/open-government-licence/version/3/

Clipart from Corel®

Printed by Zenith Print & Packaging Ltd, Pontypridd.

Based on the classic CGP style created by Richard Parsons.

Text, design, layout and original illustrations
© Coordination Group Publications Ltd. (CGP) 2019
All rights reserved.

How to Use this Book

- This book contains <u>36 workouts</u>. We've split them into <u>3 sections</u>, one for each term, with <u>12 workouts</u> each. There's roughly one workout for <u>every week</u> of the school year.

- Each workout is out of <u>12 marks</u> and should take about <u>10 minutes</u>.

- Each workout tests at least one <u>spelling objective</u> (from the government's <u>programme of study</u>) and a <u>vocabulary topic</u>. The vocabulary questions aim to introduce pupils to <u>new words</u> and expand their <u>vocabularies</u>.

- Pupils may not know all the vocabulary words. Encourage them to use <u>context</u>, or a <u>dictionary</u> where necessary, to work out unfamiliar words.

- Each workout ends with a fun <u>puzzle</u> to challenge pupils.

- The <u>first 3 workouts</u> in the Autumn Term test <u>Year 5 spelling content</u> and easier <u>vocabulary</u> — they're ideal for <u>reminding</u> pupils what they learnt in the <u>previous year</u>. These should be done at the <u>start</u> of Year 6.

- The <u>last 6 workouts</u> only contain <u>Year 6 spelling content</u> and they test harder <u>vocabulary</u>. They should be done at the <u>end</u> of Year 6.

- The other workouts contain a <u>mix</u> of <u>old</u> and <u>new</u> topics.
  As the book progresses, the tests increase in <u>difficulty</u>.

- <u>Answers</u> and a <u>progress chart</u> can be found at the <u>back</u> of the book.

The <u>contents page</u> will help you identify which statutory <u>spelling</u> requirement and <u>vocabulary topic</u> are being tested in each workout. You can use these to pick the workout which best <u>suits</u> you and the needs of your class (but remember the <u>later</u> in the book, the <u>harder</u> the workout will be, so it's best to save the workouts towards the end of the book for <u>later in the year</u>).

There is a <u>tick box</u> next to each workout on the contents page. Use this to <u>record</u> which tests have been attempted. You can also use the <u>progress chart</u> to track pupils' scores.

Contents — Autumn Term

Contents — Spring Term

Contents — Summer Term

Spelling Practice

1. Circle the correct spelling of the words in **bold** below.

    The car was made out of **steal** / **steel**.

    Ruth wanted **advice** / **advise** on which car to buy.

    We had an unexpected **guessed** / **guest** for dinner.

    The show had incredible special **affects** / **effects**.

    Chanan had always hated reading **aloud** / **allowed**.

    5 marks

Vocabulary Questions

2. Read the text below.

    > The jungle was so **dense** that I could barely see where I was going. I crept on **tentatively**, trying to find my way through the **unfamiliar territory**. I couldn't help thinking about all of the dangers that might lie round the next corner, and I was becoming more and more **unsettled**.

    What do you think the words in **bold** mean?
    Circle the word you think is the best match.

    a) **dense**   scary / thick / vast

    1 mark

    b) **tentatively**   quickly / excitedly / cautiously

    1 mark

c) **unfamiliar**   unknown / unforgiving / unusual

1 mark

d) **territory**   land / fear / breeze

1 mark

e) **unsettled**   weary / agitated / interested

1 mark

3. Write a sentence of your own using **two**
    of the words in **bold** from Question 2.

....

....

2 marks

How did you do?

Score:

Puzzle: Jungle Crossword

Use the clues to work out the jungle words.

Across:

2. The place where an animal lives

4. Noise made by leaves moving in the wind

5. Animals at risk are called ... species.

Down:

1. Extremely hot

2. Snake bites can be very ...

3. Jungle animals are ... than pets.

Puzzle Complete? ✓

Spelling Practice

1. Complete the words in **bold** by adding '**ent**' or '**ant**'.

    Kat longed to travel to a **dist**.......... land.

    The **Anci**.......... Egyptians built the pyramids.

    Zunaira wanted to be **independ**.......... .

    The **vali**.......... knight rode into battle.

    The criminal claimed he was **innoc**.......... .

5 marks

Vocabulary Questions

2. Give **two synonyms** for each word below.

    good

    ....

    ....

    bad

    ....

    ....

4 marks

3. Replace each word in **bold** with a synonym
    to make the passage more interesting.

I had a **great** .... time this weekend. We got a

train into the city and went to the aquarium. We saw so many

interesting .... sea creatures but my favourite

was the shark. It was very **fun** ....

3 marks

How did you do?

Score:

Puzzle: Water Words

Unscramble the words below and match them to a synonym.
All the words have something to do with water.

Puzzle Complete?

Spelling Practice

1. Write the correct spelling of the words in **bold** on the lines.

   I **recieved** a chemistry set for Christmas. ....

   The robber was known to be **decietful**. ....

   The **preist** tried to live a simple life. ....

   The shopkeeper handed me the **reciept**. ....

   Henry went to **retreeve** the ball. ....

   It was a **releif** when we won. ....

   6 marks

Vocabulary Questions

2. Use a **dictionary** to find out the meaning of these adjectives.

   inconsolable

   ....

   exasperated

   ....

   petrified

   ....

   3 marks

3. Complete each sentence using a word in **bold**
from Question 2. Use each word once.

a) They were so .... as the
   monster came towards them that they screamed.

1 mark

b) John was .... by his
   little brother's irritating behaviour.

1 mark

c) Claire was .... when she
   lost her necklace — she couldn't stop crying.

1 mark

How did you do?

Score:

Puzzle: Puzzling Emotions

You are a secret agent who has just been assigned a new code name.
Unscramble the words in bold and write them in the grid.
The letters in the shaded boxes spell out the code name.

1. He was **escatitc** that he won.

2. She was **axniuos** before the exam.

3. She was **egera** to do a good job.

4. I was **lnleoy** because my friends were away.

5. He is **trierifed** of spiders.

Your code name is: ....

Puzzle Complete?

Spelling Practice

1. Unscramble the words in **purple**.
    Use the clues in black to help you.

    a place to exercise: **myg** ....

    a story that might not be true: **thym** ....

    something unsolved: **restmyy** ....

    an Ancient Egyptian building: **paydrim** ....

    a word that means the
    same as another: **mysonny** ....

    5 marks

Vocabulary Questions

2. Read the text below.

> As Andre entered the shop, he immediately felt
> **overwhelmed** by how big it was. Hundreds of antiques
> were balanced **precariously** on shelves and **littered**
> across the shop floor. The **unkempt** shopkeeper
> strongly resembled an old scarecrow, and the desk he sat
> behind was **swamped** with stacks of books and paper.

What do you think the words in **purple** mean?
Circle the word you think is the best match.

If you're not sure, use a dictionary to help you.

a) **overwhelmed**   happy / stunned / lucky

    1 mark

8

b) **precariously**   unsafely / safely / neatly

1 mark

c) **littered**   boxed / scattered / wasted

1 mark

d) **unkempt**   scruffy / shy / suspicious

1 mark

e) **swamped**   cracked / damp / crowded

1 mark

3. Write a sentence of your own using **two** of these words.

....

....

2 marks

How did you do?   **Score:**

Puzzle: Complete The Words

Use the clues to work out the words.

Across:

2. Unclear or lacking detail

4. An old and valuable collectible

6. Not like anything else

Down:

1. A feeling of extreme tiredness

3. A group of sports teams who compete against each other

5. A muscle in the mouth used for tasting

Spelling Practice

1. Complete the words in **bold** by adding 'cious' or 'tious'.

    a) The wolves are very **vi**.............. .

    1 mark

    b) My grandma drives slowly on the
        motorway, as she is very **cau**.............. .

    1 mark

    c) The fragrant casserole tastes **deli**.............. .

    1 mark

    d) Washing your hands helps to
        avoid **infec**.............. diseases.

    1 mark

    e) Tia did not recognise the woman
        so she started to feel **suspi**.............. .

    1 mark

    f) Tariq reluctantly ate some **nutri**.............. fruit.

    1 mark

Vocabulary Questions

2. For each word in **bold**, write a more interesting word.

    Sasha finds video games **fun**.   ....

    Adrian finds exercising **hard**.   ....

    Pam thought the film was **funny**.   ....

    3 marks

3. Josiah has written about his first day at his new school.
   Replace the words in **bold** with more interesting words.

This morning, I had a lengthy conversation with a

nice .... boy who sits next to me. He said

he felt extremely **silly** .... because his mum

kissed him goodbye in front of his friends! Then the

bell rang and a teacher silently entered the classroom.

I gulped — she looked incredibly **scary** ....

3 marks

How did you do?

Score:

Puzzle: Pyramid Puzzle

Each new word in the pyramid is made up of the letters from the
word above it, plus the new letter on the left. Work out what
each new word should be, using the clues on the right to help you.

Letters		Clue
I N		
add a P		attach to a board
add an S		turn around quickly
add an E		backbone
add an O		small horses
add a G		birds you often see in cities
add an X		uncovering or revealing

Puzzle Complete? ✓

11

Autumn Term: Workout 6

Spelling Practice

1. Circle the correct spelling of the words in **bold** below.

    Coco felt very **speshul / special** on her birthday.

    It's **essential / essencial** to bring sun cream on holiday.

    Monkeys are friendly, **sosial / social** animals.

    The top secret letter was strictly
    confidenshal / confidential.

    The young girl had the **potential / potencial**
    to be an amazing singer.

    ____
    5 marks

Vocabulary Questions

2. Complete each sentence with a synonym of the word in **bold**.

    The nurse soothed the **worried** .... patient.

    The ambulance **sped** ....
    past other cars, its lights flashing brightly.

    The doctor **permitted** ....
    the unwell woman to go for a walk.

    ____
    3 marks

12

3. Complete this letter using the words from the box.
    Use each word once.

> questionnaire   hospital   appointment   confirm

Dear Mr Mahmood,

I am writing to .... your

.... on Thursday 15th May at 09:15.

Please arrive at the .... at least 10

minutes beforehand, as we will require you to fill out a

short .... before seeing the doctor.

4 marks

How did you do?

Score:

Puzzle: Missing Link

For each row, find a word that can be
added to the end of the word on the left
and the start of the word on the right.

SPACE	S				WRECK
CAMP			R		MAN
FOOT			L		ROOM
POP				N	FLAKE
FAMILY				E	HOUSE

From top to bottom,
what word is written
in the shaded boxes?

....

Puzzle Complete? 

Spelling Practice

1. Complete the words in **bold** by adding
    '**sion**', '**ssion**', '**tion**', '**ation**' or '**cian**'.

    The new parents looked at their baby with **ador**............ .

    Adjoa preferred **divi**............ to multiplication.

    The class had a **discu**............ about pets.

    The **politi**............ made his speech to the crowd.

    Noah used to love reading **fic**............ books.

    5 marks

Vocabulary Questions

2. Read the passage below.

> The Grand Canyon is an enormous **gorge** in the United States.
> It was formed by the Colorado River, which has been **flowing**
> through the **landscape** for millions of years. The water has
> **persistently** cut away at the rock, creating a canyon that **spans**
> 18 miles across in some places. The river continues to **erode** the
> rock, **changing** the shape of the Grand Canyon even today.

Use a **dictionary** to find out the meaning of the words in **purple**.
Circle the word you think is the best match.

a) **gorge**   valley / stone / mountain

1 mark

b) **persistently**   carefully / continually / quickly

1 mark

c) **spans**   weighs / reaches / seems

d) **erode**   settle / neglect / destroy

3. Use a **thesaurus** to find more interesting words
    for the words in **black** from the passage.

flowing   ....

landscape   ....

changing   ....

How did you do?   **Score:**

Puzzle: Rock Crossword

Use the clues to work out the rock-related words.

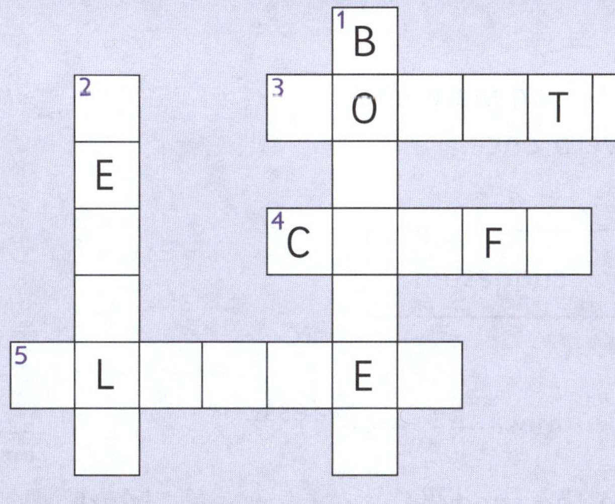

Across:

3. Something you climb
that's taller than a hill

4. A very steep rock face

5. Someone who clambers
up hills or rocks

Down:

1. A very large rock

2. A small stone

Puzzle Complete? 

Autumn Term: Workout 7

Autumn Term: Workout 8

Spelling Practice

1. Complete the words in **bold** by adding
    'ance', 'ancy', 'ence' or 'ency'.

    Miss Shah tried to teach them **toler**......................... .

    There is a job **vac**......................... in my local takeaway.

    The pilot made an **emerg**......................... landing.

    The detective needed **evid**......................... .

    The popstar was known for his **arrog**......................... .

    5 marks

Vocabulary Questions

2. Choose a verb from the box to complete each
    of the sentences. Use each verb once.

confided   snapped   suggested

    a) "It's your fault we lost it!" .... Jess.

    1 mark

    b) "Perhaps we could look in the shed?" .... Mark.

    1 mark

    c) "I have a secret," .... Olivia.

    1 mark

16

3. Replace the word '**said**' in the story below to make it more interesting. Use a different verb each time.

"Where were you the night the amulets were stolen from the museum?" **said** .... the inspector.

"I was out with work colleagues. You can check with them," **said** .... Alastair.

"That's funny," **said** .... the inspector, "because we have evidence to the contrary."

"Impossible!" **said** .... Alastair, with a menacing gleam in his eyes.

4 marks

How did you do?

Score:

Spelling Practice

1. Circle the correct spelling of the words in **bold**.

    There is a lot of **caffiene / caffeine** in coffee.

    Rebecca was **anxious / ancious** to see the new film.

    Viraj went with his **inicial / initial** decision.

    I am always happy to give you **assistance / assistence**.

    It was a beautiful **provintial / provincial** town.

    5 marks

Vocabulary Questions

2. Look at the pictures. Write down **two** interesting **adjectives** to describe each setting.

    ....

    ....

    ....

    ....

    4 marks

3. Use a **thesaurus** to replace the words
    in **bold** in the sentences below.

    It was **peaceful** in the mountains.   ....

    The prison cell was **gloomy**.   ....

    London is very **busy** today.   ....

                                                                    3 marks

How did you do?   Score:

Puzzle: Word Pyramids

Each new word in the pyramid is made up of the letters from the
word above it, plus the new letter on the left. Work out what each
new word should be, using the clues on the right to help you.

	P R E Y	an animal that is hunted
add a C	P E R C Y	a boys' name
add an E	C R E E P Y	scary

	O R	either
add a U		belonging to us
add an H		60 minutes
add a G		opposite of smooth

	T E N	eight, nine, ...
add a D		take care of
add an R		a new fashion
add an E		kind and caring

Puzzle Complete? ✓

Autumn Term: Workout 9

Autumn Term: Workout 10

Spelling Practice

1. Circle the correct spelling of the words in **bold**.

   You need to practise if you want to **impruve** / **improve**.

   It was very **buzy** / **busy** in London today.

   We saw a sea monster in the **water** / **warter**.

   The film was two **ours** / **hours** long.

   It was a **beutiful** / **beautiful** day today.

   I want to buy some new **clothes** / **cloaths** for the party. ____

   6 marks

Vocabulary Questions

2. Use a **dictionary** to find out the meaning of the words below.

   exhilarated

   ....

   preoccupied

   ....

   despondent

   ....

   3 marks

3. Complete each sentence using a word in **bold** from Question 2.

The artist was very quiet — she wasn't unhappy,

just ....

Lena felt .... after

receiving thunderous applause.

His defeat had left him completely ....

3 marks

How did you do?

Score:

Puzzle: Corrections Crossword

Underline the misspelt word in each sentence,
then write the correct spelling in the crossword.

Across:

5. The bears have broken into our garden agen.

6. Evrybody is away next week, so we should postpone the party.

Down:

1. I practise becos I want to be a professional musician.

2. The recipe requires flour, shugar and eggs.

3. It is extremely hard to clime Mount Everest.

4. We onely bought eight tickets.

Puzzle Complete? 

21

Autumn Term: Workout 11

Spelling Practice

1. Write the correct spelling of the words in **bold** on the lines.

   Rob had **forgoten** his lunch again.   ....

   Neha spends her Sundays **gardenning**.   ....

   The **referree** blew the final whistle.   ....

   I am taking a **beginers'** French class.   ....

   The dog **prefered** steak to poultry.   ....

   5 marks

Vocabulary Questions

2. Draw lines to match each word with an **antonym**.

   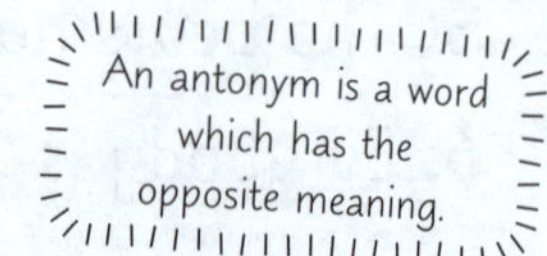

   rich   immaculate   conscientious

   careless   destitute   scruffy

   2 marks

3. Replace each word in **bold** with an **antonym**
   to change the meaning of the sentence.

   a) Hedgehogs are **common** .... in this area.

   1 mark

   b) The books in the library were **ancient** ....

   1 mark

22

c) The sea was very **still** ....
when we were on the cruise.

1 mark

d) The exchange student was **courteous** ....
to the host family.

1 mark

e) We had **insufficient** .... supplies
to get us through the long journey.

1 mark

How did you do?

Score:

Puzzle: Antonym Wordsearch

Find the antonyms of the words below in the wordsearch.

Word	**Antonym**
deep	....
safe	....
positive	....
create	....
blunt	....
lowest	....
ancient	....

A	E	D	E	S	T	R	O	Y	A	S
S	H	A	R	P	X	B	U	P	D	M
O	E	N	W	S	V	H	J	K	P	O
A	S	G	G	H	N	M	R	E	F	D
S	N	E	G	A	T	I	V	E	K	E
P	F	R	I	L	D	X	O	U	E	R
Y	D	O	H	L	J	E	R	O	G	N
J	D	U	U	O	K	F	M	L	H	U
D	U	S	I	W	R	H	E	N	W	V
W	R	H	I	G	H	E	S	T	F	I

Puzzle Complete? ✓

23

Spelling Practice

1. Circle the correct spelling of the words in **bold**.

    The new house is **consideribly / considerably** larger.

    The weather is **changable / changeable** in England.

    The cake decorations are **edible / edable**.

    The baby kangaroo is **adoreable / adorable**.

    It was **terribly / terrably** crowded on the bus.

    5 marks

Vocabulary Questions

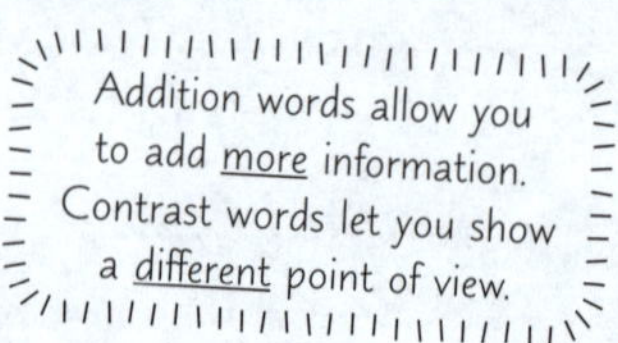

2. Sort the words in the box below into '**addition**' words and '**contrast**' words.

moreover	conversely
furthermore	however

Addition words: **Contrast** words:

....

....

4 marks

24

3. Complete the text below using words from Question 2.

Learning another language can help you find out information

while you're on holiday. ...., it gives

you the chance to befriend people you wouldn't normally

speak to. ...., it can be fun to learn

a language. ...., many people don't

find it fun because learning a language can be difficult.

3 marks

How did you do?

Score:

Puzzle: Word Wheel

Adil is on a game show and needs your help to win.
Find as many words as you can using the letters in the
wheel below. Each word must contain the letter E.

0-4 words: Keep going, he's relying on you!

5-9 words: Looking good... can you spot any more?

10-14 words: Great job — don't stop now!

15+ words: Fantastic — Adil's won the game!

Bonus: Can you find the nine-letter word? ....

Puzzle Complete? 

Spring Term: Workout 1

Spelling Practice

1. Add a **prefix** to the words in **bold** so each
    sentence means the opposite.

    Luna watched the car **appear**. ....

    Max thought the girl's voice was **familiar**. ....

    Mr Khan gave us the **correct** answers. ....

    John thought flying cars were **possible**. ....

    Our pet cat knows how to **behave**. ....

    5 marks

Vocabulary Questions

2. Read the text below.

As an archaeologist, Olga had to spend many tedious hours **looking**
at dusty **tomes**. However, she also saw lots of **interesting** ruins.
When **searching** these ruins, she **unearthed** precious **things**.
"I have the best job in the world!" she often **said**.

Look up the following words from the passage in a
dictionary. Using the dictionary definition to help you,
write down another word with a **similar meaning**.

a) **tome** ....

1 mark

b) **unearthed** ....

1 mark

3. Use a **thesaurus** to find more interesting words
    for the words in **purple** from the passage.

looking   ....

interesting   ....

searching   ....

things   ....

said   ....

5 marks

How did you do?

Score:

Puzzle: Ancient Crossword

Use the clues to work out
the history words.

Across:

4. Where people are buried

6. Remains of a creature
   preserved in stone

7. Person or thing carved
   out of stone

Down:

1. History is the study of the ...

2. Where a monarch lives

3. Buildings which are
   now destroyed

5. When interesting things are
   found they are often put here

Puzzle Complete? 

Spring Term: Workout 2

Spelling Practice

1. Underline the words that are spelt incorrectly
    and write the correct spellings on the lines.

    Alan wanted to interrupt and tell her not to exagerate.

    ....

    Taking the aggressive rhino on the boat was a disastrus idea.

    ....

    Erin started a comittee to work on saving the environment.

    ....

    6 marks

Vocabulary Questions

2. Use a **thesaurus** to find a
    synonym for the words below.

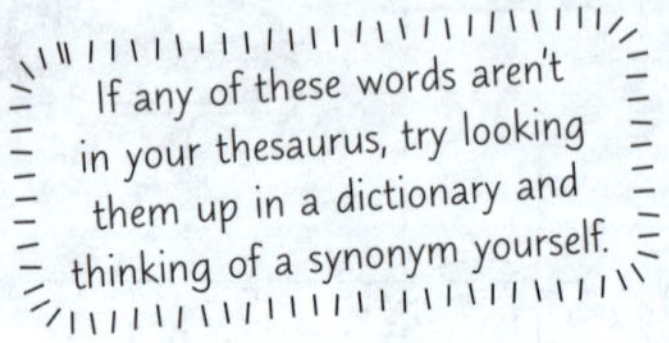

    dilapidated   ....

    malevolent   ....

    ghastly   ....

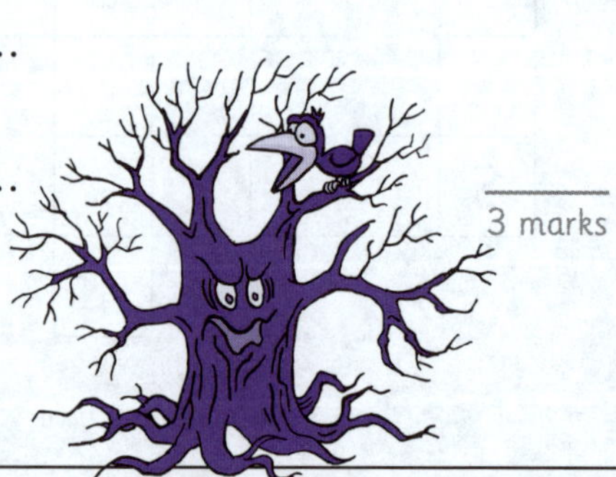

3 marks

3. Make this horror story more interesting by adding in the words in **bold** from Question 2. Use each word once.

As I stumbled through the dark forest, I could sense a

.... presence watching me. Eventually,

I came to a .... cabin. I was about to

enter when I heard a .... scream.

3 marks

How did you do?

Score:

Spelling Practice

1. Complete the words in **bold** by adding in the correct **silent letter**.

The quiz included a general .... **nowledge** round.

Charlie decided to take up **balle** .... lessons.

The race car driver **fas** .... **ened** her seat belt.

We had to call a **plum** .... **er** to fix the sink.

The **i** .... **land** was covered in palm trees.

5 marks

Vocabulary Questions

2. Complete the diary entry below using the words from the box. Use each word once.

vicious	docile	inquisitively	razor-sharp	waddling

Today we paid a visit to the zoo. I was terrified of the lion because it looked .... The crocodile also had .... teeth. The giraffe seemed very .... as it quietly ate some leaves. At midday, we saw a penguin parade .... through the zoo. We then visited the meerkats, which stared at us .... as if we were the zoo animals, not them.

5 marks

30

3.   Use a **thesaurus** to replace the words in **bold** in the text.

Jonah and Gill set off for the animal shelter with their parents. When they arrived, a puppy **ran** .... over to them and licked their faces. He seemed like a very **energetic** .... dog indeed.

2 marks

How did you do?

Score:

Puzzle: Animal Wordsearch

Unscramble the words and find them in the wordsearch.

1. Bears **hbinretae** during the winter.

2. Donkeys are known to be **dcolie** animals.

3. The eagle **saroed** through the valley.

4. Penguins are **apadetd** to their environment.

5. The deer **panrecd** through the meadow.

6. The wolves **hwoeld** all night long.

7. The lion is a **cranviroe**.

A	G	Y	H	U	G	B	S	E	J	I
D	F	J	U	O	I	O	P	Z	E	H
E	F	J	K	O	W	F	G	T	C	I
O	U	V	G	U	K	L	M	K	A	B
W	S	O	A	R	E	D	E	A	R	E
S	D	F	J	U	E	C	X	D	N	R
Z	V	D	O	C	I	L	E	A	I	N
D	S	W	N	B	N	Y	K	L	V	A
S	E	A	I	U	N	I	N	G	O	T
E	R	F	G	J	I	N	N	E	R	E
P	Q	F	H	A	D	A	P	T	E	D

Puzzle Complete? 

31

Spelling Practice

1. Unscramble the words in **purple**.
    Use the words in black to help you.

    All of the words end in 'ly'.

    With spite: **stiepflluy** ....

    With arrogance: **aorrnaglty** ....

    With venom: **vonemusoyl** ....

    With malice: **mlicaousily** ....

    With courage: **curoegausloy** ....

    5 marks

Vocabulary Questions

2. Complete each sentence with a synonym of the adverb in **bold**.

    Cara was awarded the medal for acting **heroically**
    .... in the face of danger.

    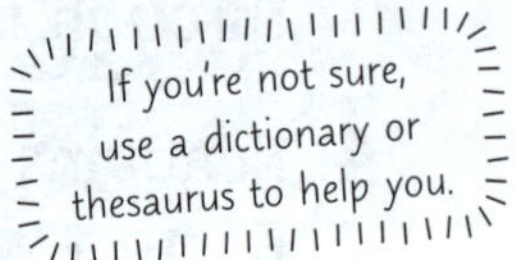

    If you're not sure, use a dictionary or thesaurus to help you.

    Mario had hurt his back, so he sat down
    very **gingerly** ....

    Shanice looked up **apprehensively**
    .... when she
    heard her name being shouted.

    3 marks

32

3. Complete the sentences using the words in the box.
Use each word once.

| generously   vigorously   ingeniously   gradually |

Marcus gave .... to charity.

Mo shook the bottle .... until it exploded.

Tim was .... becoming
more confident with his driving.

Alice had .... invented a
device which would tidy her room for her.

4 marks

How did you do?

Score:

Puzzle: Detective's Assistant

There's been a robbery! Use the picture clues to work
out the missing words and solve the crime.

CLUE: The missing words are homophones of the pictures.

The robbery happened at  .... According to our

 .... of information, the thief stole £1000. Witnesses reported

seeing a .... white van waiting outside the bank. It is

believed the thief has fled abroad, possibly to the  ....

Puzzle Complete? 

Spring Term: Workout 5

Spelling Practice

1. Circle the correct words to complete the sentences.

The priest placed the book on the **altar / alter**.

There's a **draft / draught** coming in through the open door.

I'll ask my mum to **altar / alter** my dress before the party.

The new system won't **affect / effect** people over 25.

The writer finished her first **draft / draught** of the novel.

Regular exercise has a positive **affect / effect** on your mind. _______

6 marks

Vocabulary Questions

2. Use a **dictionary** to look up the meaning of each **verb** in the box. Then complete the sentences below, using each word once.

contract	prophesy	attribute
patrol	permit	complement

a) The fortune teller will .... my future. _______

1 mark

b) He likes to .... the grounds regularly. _______

1 mark

c) The flavours in the meal .... each other. _______

1 mark

d) I .... my success to my family.

1 mark

e) He didn't want to .... the disease.

1 mark

f) My mum won't .... me to eat sweets.

1 mark

How did you do?

Score:

Puzzle: Personality Wordsearch

Find six words in the grid that you could use to describe someone. Then think of a synonym for each word.

1. Word: ....

Synonym: ....

2. Word: ....

Synonym: ....

3. Word: ....

Synonym: ....

4. Word: ....

Synonym: ....

5. Word: ....

Synonym: ....

W	Y	U	S	D	E	N	C	E	J	F
P	Q	D	B	F	U	L	R	R	L	G
R	E	L	I	A	B	L	E	H	E	B
J	M	O	D	E	S	T	A	Y	U	N
X	V	K	H	Y	S	R	T	I	S	J
F	N	G	B	N	U	O	I	N	J	K
C	A	R	I	N	G	F	V	G	O	L
T	S	V	P	U	F	K	E	F	L	I
S	T	R	E	H	U	Y	K	D	I	O
X	Y	K	T	E	M	G	N	K	S	W
C	V	G	T	N	G	Y	I	U	W	S

Puzzle Complete? ✓

35

Spring Term: Workout 5

Spring Term: Workout 6

Spelling Practice

1. Add a **hyphen** in the correct position to each of the words **below**.

cooperate   coown

reevaluate   reenter

prearrange   preorder

6 marks

Vocabulary Questions

2. What do you think the phrases in **bold** mean? Circle the best match.

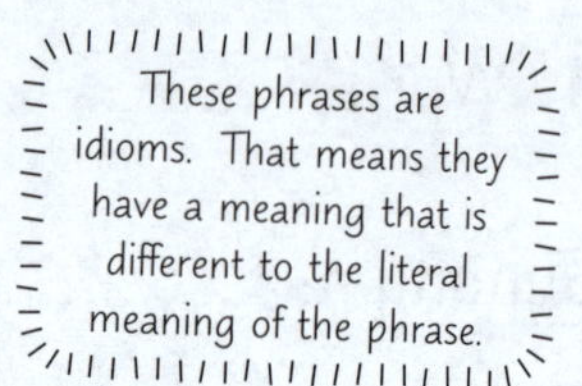

a) Joanne was feeling **under the weather** for a few days.

wet and cold / unwell / lively

1 mark

b) Abed thought his new bat was **the bee's knees**.

worst / most painful / brilliant

1 mark

c) Liv was **on top of the world** when she got her exam results.

thrilled / nervous / dizzy

1 mark

d) Katya's new car had cost her **an arm and a leg**.

a penny / a lot of money / her health

1 mark

e) It was **raining cats and dogs** on Thursday!

very busy / raining heavily / very noisy

1 mark

f) Shane **hit the nail on the head** with his explanation.

was exactly right / attracted attention / sent a message

1 mark

How did you do?

Score:

Puzzle: Mixed Messages

Unscramble the words in bold in the match report below to find out how CGP United played at the weekend.

CGP United **dminoaetd** the **opsopoitin** in their match on Saturday. They played **sprebluy** and their **blirlancie** lasted for the whole 90 minutes. They were by far the **sprueoir** team.

1. ....

2. ....

3. ....

4. ....

5. ....

Do you think they won? ....

Puzzle Complete? 

37

Spelling Practice

1. Underline the words that are spelt incorrectly and write the correct spellings on the lines.

    He had to flee the contry immediately. ....

    Lena finished the dance with a florish. ....

    The ocean was extremely rugh that day. ....

    6 marks

Vocabulary Questions

2. Read the text below.

> Elsa was exhausted as she **clambered** up the rocky volcano. After a tough climb, she pulled herself onto a plateau, where nature was thriving. As she slowly **meandered** through the grass, a small movement caught her eye. She bent down to see dozens of small mice **scurrying** away from the summit. Her heart sank as a deafening roar **reverberated** through the valley.

What do you think the verbs in **purple** mean?
Circle the word you think is the best match.

a) **clambered**   walked / climbed / slid

1 mark

b) **meandered**   hurried / wandered / jumped

1 mark

c) **scurrying**   dashing / worrying / hiding

1 mark

d) **reverberated**   echoed / sang / soared

1 mark

3.   Write a sentence of your own using **two**
     of the words in **bold** from Question 2.

....

....

2 marks

How did you do?   Score: [   ]

Puzzle: Adventure Verbs Wordsearch

Unscramble the adventure words in the sentences
and find them in the wordsearch below.

1. They **sgletrugd** on
   through the blizzard.

2. He **trpsiaed** across
   the desert.

3. They had to
   itnsnefiy their
   search.

4. She **srcmbaeld**
   down the cliff face.

5. He **wertlsed** his
   bag from the lion.

6. We **saenekd**
   through the cave.

R	T	C	D	R	J	U	I	A	U	S
W	R	E	S	T	L	E	D	F	G	T
E	A	Y	T	J	I	P	Z	M	V	R
Q	I	N	T	E	N	S	I	F	Y	U
S	P	F	G	H	U	J	V	E	R	G
P	S	N	E	A	K	E	D	O	R	G
C	E	G	H	Y	J	U	O	W	E	L
S	D	E	G	H	B	V	I	Y	N	E
S	C	R	A	M	B	L	E	D	E	D

Puzzle Complete?

39

10

Spelling Practice

1. Tick the sentences below that use apostrophes correctly.

   ☐ Myriam couldn't find her mices' favourite food.

   ☐ All three girls' pencils needed sharpening immediately.

   ☐ The children's favourite game was noughts and crosses.

   2 marks

2. Put apostrophes in the correct places below.

   Four vans engines were abandoned in the yard.

   The teachers were getting ready for parents evening.

   Witches spells are usually written in rhyme.

   3 marks

Vocabulary Questions

3. Use a **dictionary** to find out the meanings of the adjectives below.

   advantageous ....

   prestigious ....

   exceptional ....

   thrilling ....

   4 marks

4. Complete each sentence using a word in **bold** from Question 3. Do not use a word more than once.

The new supermarket will be .... to all of us.

The dancers put on an .... performance.

The actress received the most ....
award at the ceremony.

3 marks

How did you do?

Score:

Puzzle: Unscramble And Search

Unscramble the words below and find them in the wordsearch.

1. Before it lands, a plane has to **dnecesd**.

2. Mitch loved learning about **sincece**.

3. The pig was **fsaednctai** by mud.

4. Sona pulled a **mslcue** while running.

5. Gavin was prepared to **acnsed** the mountain.

6. The island had some beautiful **snrecey**.

Y	U	D	E	G	H	U	I	N	B
M	T	E	D	V	I	B	N	R	Z
J	U	K	Q	R	D	E	I	K	C
I	N	S	S	F	G	L	L	D	O
F	A	S	C	I	N	A	T	E	D
R	K	J	I	L	M	E	J	S	N
I	Q	C	E	Z	E	M	R	C	E
C	E	P	N	I	W	G	K	E	C
N	G	M	C	G	K	X	I	N	S
R	S	C	E	N	E	R	Y	D	A

Puzzle Complete?

Spring Term: Workout 9

Spelling Practice

1. Circle the correct spelling of the words in **bold**.

    The meat is much **tougher / tuffer** than I expected.

    The boy was sent home for being **noughty / naughty**.

    The owl was perched on the **bough / bow** of the tree.

    The two boxers **fought / fort** for twelve rounds.

    The rabbit tunnelled its way into the **borough / burrow**.

    _____
    5 marks

Vocabulary Questions

2. Use a **thesaurus** to find a **synonym** for each word below.

    If any of these words aren't in your thesaurus, try looking them up in a dictionary and thinking of a synonym yourself.

    disgusting   ....

    deadly   ....

    subterranean   ....

    _____
    3 marks

3. Write a sentence of your own using one of the words in **bold** from Question 2.

    ....

    ....

    _____
    1 mark

42

4. Write down **three adjectives** to
    describe the insect in the picture.

    ....

    ....

    ....

How did you do?   **Score:**

Puzzle: Creepy-Crawly Crossword

Use the clues to work out the creepy-crawly words.

Across:

1. An eight-legged creature

4. Scientists use this to study
tiny bugs and germs

5. The environment
an animal lives in

7. Active at night

Down:

2. Harmful to eat

3. An animal that preys
on other animals

6. Sticky like a slug

Puzzle Complete?

43

Spring Term: Workout 9

Spring Term: Workout 10

Spelling Practice

1. Unscramble the words in **bold**.

    The **cmeetrey** was eerie.

    We need to save the **evinnornmet**.

    Mudit loved sailing his **yhcat**.

    Isla asked her **sceterray** to do it.

    The **lhgiintng** lit up the sky.

    I am not **falmiiar** with that book.

    6 marks

Vocabulary Questions

2. Use a **dictionary** to find out the meanings of the words below.

    abundant

    ....

    pristine

    ....

    temperate

    ....

    3 marks

3. Complete each sentence using a word in **bold**
from Question 2. Use each word once.

The forest was in a .... climate.

The snow was .... because we
were the first people to walk on it.

Wildflowers were .... on the tropical island.

3 marks

How did you do?

Score:

E	V	E	R	G	R	E	E	N	W
T	Y	S	F	L	V	S	O	P	I
C	T	E	G	A	F	E	D	N	L
X	A	Q	L	C	L	N	U	P	D
W	F	O	L	I	A	G	E	I	E
S	F	B	T	E	M	K	L	O	R
K	B	R	E	R	A	D	F	H	N
A	E	F	G	Y	J	O	E	R	E
F	Z	E	N	H	L	U	S	H	S
P	E	A	C	E	F	U	L	R	S
S	F	I	O	F	G	Y	A	D	C

1. The meadow was **lsuh** and green.

2. There were berries growing in the **floaige**.

3. It's easy to grow things in **freitle** soil.

4. **Eervgeern** trees don't lose their leaves in winter.

5. There was an icy **gacleir** on the mountain.

6. It was **pceafuel** in the countryside.

7. There are few people in the **wlidnreses**.

Puzzle Complete? 

Spring Term: Workout 11

Spelling Practice

1. Circle the correct spelling of the words in **bold**.

   The spy accepted the top secret **mition / mission**.

   Tim watched the king's **coronation / coronashion** on TV.

   Mia wanted to be a **polititian / politician** when she grew up.

   The **animation / animatian** in the film was very impressive.

   The **magitian / magician** lived in a secret cave.

   Sarah could sense the **tention / tension** in the room.

   ____
   6 marks

Vocabulary Questions

2. Complete the text below using the **onomatopoeic** words from the box.

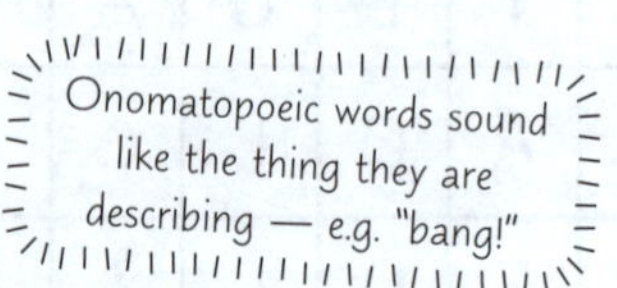

rumble	chattering	crackling	trickle

We had picked the perfect place to camp. The

birds were .... and we

could hear the gentle ....

of the stream nearby. The fire was

.... away as we warmed

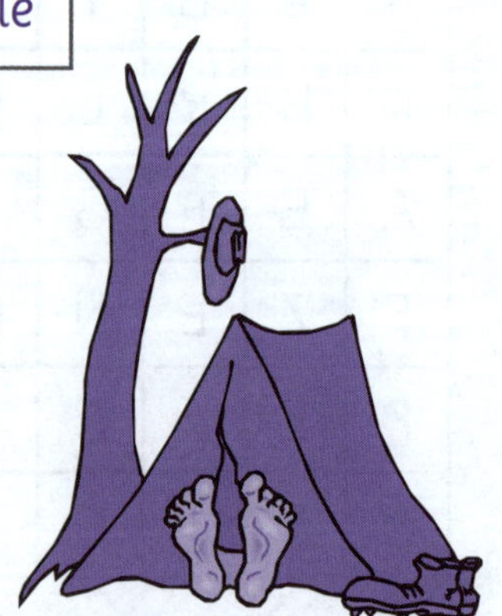

46

our hands by it. We were just about to put up the tents when we heard the distant .... of thunder.

4 marks

3.   Write a **synonym** for each word below.

bellow   ....

screech   ....

2 marks

How did you do?   **Score:** [ ]

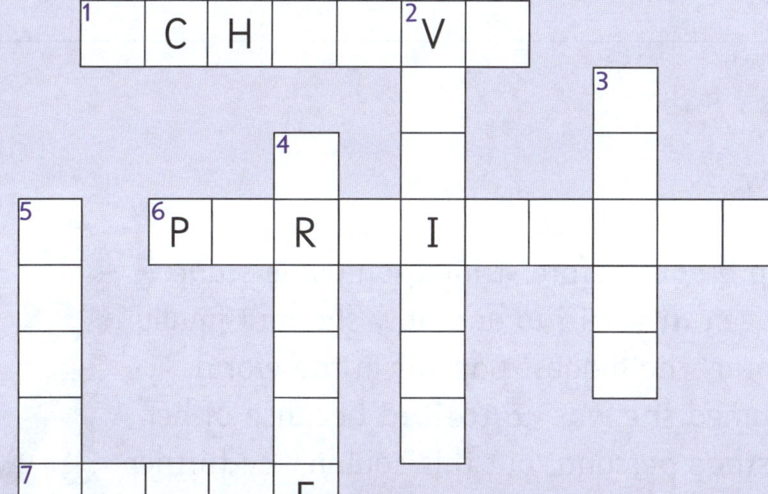

Puzzle: Complete The Words

Use the clues to complete the crossword.

Across:

1. I work hard so I can ... my aims.

6. Where laws are made

7. A technique used in poems and songs

Down:

2. There is a ... of options to choose from

3. A line of people waiting their turn

4. If you fall over you might get a ...

5. Another word for 'happen'

Puzzle Complete? 

47

Spring Term: Workout 11

Spelling Practice

1. Complete the words in **bold** by adding '**ture**' or '**sure**'.

    The mountaineers were always prepared for an **adven**.......... .

    It was chaos when the lions escaped from their **enclo**.......... .

    They couldn't identify the strange **crea**.......... in the forest.

    The legend said the pirate **trea**.......... had been lost for years.

    She hung the **pic**.......... up on the wall for everyone to see.

    _____
    5 marks

Vocabulary Questions

2. Read the text below.

    > Aimie took a deep breath before striding onto the stage. She had always been **ambitious** and now she had finally realised her dream as the biggest popstar in the world. Many people assumed she was **conceited** because of her **extravagant** onstage persona, but this couldn't be further from the truth. Aimie was still paralysed by stage fright, and her friends and family knew her to be very **modest**.

    What do you think the adjectives in **bold** mean?
    Circle the word you think is the best match.

    a) **ambitious**   shy / determined / pretentious

    _____
    1 mark

48

b)	**conceited**	arrogant / beautiful / rude	1 mark
c)	**extravagant**	subtle / popular / flamboyant	1 mark
d)	**modest**	humble / outspoken / outrageous	1 mark

3. Use a **dictionary** to find out the meaning of the words below.

shrewd ....

innovative ....

candid ....

3 marks

How did you do?

Score:

Puzzle Complete? 

Spelling Practice

1. Change the words in **bold** into **adjectives** by adding the suffix '**ous**'. You might have to change the spelling of the root words.

The north of the country is **mountain**. ....

The police officer was **courage**. ....

Miss Chu looked very **glamour**. ....

The **fame** singer gave a concert. ....

Sam was **fury** that I lost his jacket. ....

5 marks

Vocabulary Questions

2. Fill in the gaps using the words from the box.

destination	bustling	solitude	exotic

Tired of the British rain? Why not make the peaceful, ... shores of the Caribbean your next holiday ....? Stay at our new spa retreat on a **distant** island. Enjoy the .... of the quiet beaches, or go on a **trip** to the .... markets of the nearby town. Make the most of our **luxurious** swimming pool and spa facilities for no extra cost.

4 marks

50

3.   Use a **thesaurus** to find **synonyms** for these words from Q2.

distant   ....

trip   ....

luxurious   ....

How did you do?   **Score:**

Puzzle: Holiday Pyramids

Each new word in the pyramid is made up of the letters from
the word above it, plus one new letter. Work out what each
new word should be, using the clues on the right to help you.

The first one has been done for you.

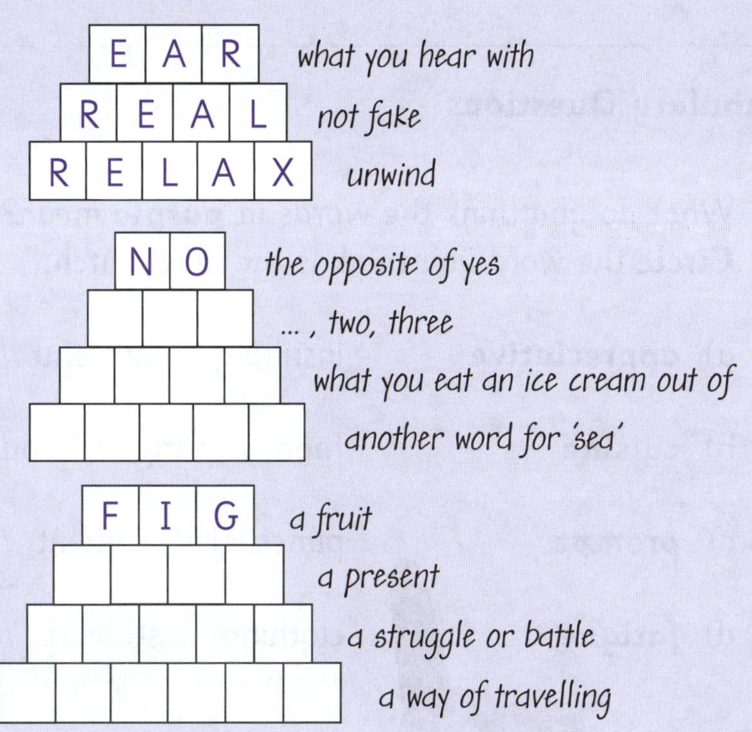

Puzzle Complete? 

51

Summer Term: Workout 2

(10)

Spelling Practice

1. Write the correct spelling of the words in **bold** on the lines.

    Tina was suffering from a bad **coff**. ....

    We built a **fought** out of pillows and sheets. ....

    We **ort** to visit grandma tomorrow. ....

    Akshay gave his room a **thora** clean. ....

    Don't **scough** at it until you've tried it. ....

    5 marks

Vocabulary Questions

2. What do you think the words in **purple** mean?
    Circle the word you think is the best match.

    If you're not sure, use a dictionary to help you.

    a) **appreciative**   insulting / grateful / enormous

    b) **cuisine**   food / party / group

    c) **prompt**   punctual / content / lucky

    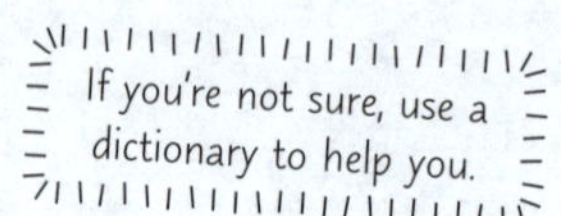

    d) **fatigue**   clothing / stability / tiredness

    4 marks

3. Read the text below. Fill in the gaps using the words in **bold** from Question 2.

Dear student,

The school is hosting an event to welcome our French exchange students. The event will begin at 4:30 pm. Traditional French .... will be served, as well as a selection of classic English snacks. We would be .... if you could be .... so we can begin on time.

3 marks

How did you do?

Score:

Puzzle: Missing Link

For each row, find a word that can be added to the end of the word on the left and the start of the word on the right.

TEXT	▓	☐	☐	☐	SHELF
TRAP	☐	☐	☐	▓	BELL
WORK	☐	☐	▓	☐	LIFT
HORSE	☐	☐	▓	☐	LACE
BED	☐	☐	☐	▓	MATE

From top to bottom, what word is written in the shaded boxes?

....

Puzzle Complete? ✓

Summer Term: Workout 2

Summer Term: Workout 3

Spelling Practice

1. Circle the correct spelling of the words in **bold**.

    Christie was sick of her friend's evil **skeming** / **scheming**.

    Bigfoot lives in a remote **chalet** / **shalet** in the mountains.

    Tanya wants to be a **chemist** / **cemist** when she grows up.

    Will jumped out of a plane with a **parashute** / **parachute**.

    The best bit of the song is the **corus** / **chorus**.

    ____
    5 marks

Vocabulary Questions

2. For each pair of **bold** words, **circle** the word
    which makes the most sense in the passage.

    Mr Hempton was relieved that the chaotic school trip was over.

    To begin with, Marion had **absentmindedly** / **efficiently**

    stepped in front of a bus, causing the bus driver to screech

    to a halt to avoid hitting the careless student. Next, Douglas

    had **cautiously** / **recklessly** run off. Luckily, Ms Simms

    managed to find him and marched him back to the

    group, looking at him **reproachfully** / **reassuringly**.

    All of this made them late, so they had to

    walk **punctually** / **briskly** to the museum.

    ____
    4 marks

3. Choose a suitable **adverb** to complete each sentence.

Rachel smiled .... at the old photo.

Bryan worked .... for the exam.

The film was .... based on a true story.

3 marks

How did you do?

Score:

Puzzle: Adverbs Wordsearch

Add a suffix to the words below to make them into adverbs, then find them in the wordsearch.

CLUE: You may need to change the spelling of the root word.

1. frantic

....

2. moderate

....

3. final

....

4. greedy

....

5. tolerable

....

6. graceful

....

F	R	A	N	T	I	C	A	L	L	Y
S	D	E	R	O	T	Y	U	I	N	G
Y	U	O	P	L	X	V	G	J	R	R
W	E	J	Y	E	V	R	I	E	O	F
M	O	D	E	R	A	T	E	L	Y	I
X	C	H	U	A	K	D	R	U	I	N
Z	X	G	J	B	I	R	Y	I	O	A
S	D	Y	U	L	J	E	I	N	K	L
A	V	G	Y	Y	P	O	Y	V	A	L
O	R	D	G	A	F	I	E	R	L	Y
G	R	A	C	E	F	U	L	L	Y	S

Puzzle Complete? ✓

Summer Term: Workout 3

55

Spelling Practice

1. **Circle** the correct spelling of the words in **bold** below.

   Henry was searching for **presious** / **precious** metals.

   Chickenpox is very **infectious** / **infecious**.

   Anaya was very **ambitious** / **ambicious**.

   The apartment was very **spasious** / **spacious**.

   The story about the dinosaur was **ficticious** / **fictitious**.

   ____
   5 marks

Vocabulary Questions

2. Draw lines to match the words to their **meanings**.

   increase   decrease   estimate   deduce

   go down   guess   figure out   go up

   ____
   3 marks

3. Replace the words and phrases in **bold** with
   verbs that have **similar meanings**.

   It is really difficult for scientists to tell when a volcano is going

   to erupt. They often **look at** .... the volcano to see if its appearance has changed. You can also **find out** .... a lot about a volcano from the number of earthquakes that happen nearby. If the number of earthquakes **goes up** .... , this sometimes means that the volcano might erupt soon. Scientists **try** .... to give people as much warning as possible.

How did you do?

4 marks

Score:

Puzzle: Complete The Words

Use the clues to complete the crossword.

Across:

3. A number

4. Lots of brides wear one of these

6. Our next-door ... looks after our cat when we are away

7. It is important to ... the rules

Down:

1. How heavy something is

2. Blood runs through your ...

5. The tiger stalked its ... through the trees

Puzzle Complete?

57

Summer Term: Workout 5

Spelling Practice

1. Add a **hyphen** in the correct position to each of the words in **bold**.

    We decided to **c o o r d i n a t e** our outfits.

    Deepak had to **r e e n t e r** the building later.

    The team had to **c o o p e r a t e** to get the work done.

    Taylor and Paige **c o o w n** the company.

    The scientists had to **r e e v a l u a t e** their methods.

    5 marks

Vocabulary Questions

2. Read the news report below.

    > A priceless painting has been stolen from a local art gallery. The **unprecedented** incident occurred on Tuesday. One person was **detained** on suspicion of aiding in the robbery but was later released. The theft is **allegedly** the work of **infamous** thief Andy Watson. Chief Inspector Jenny Chambers today reminded the public to stay **vigilant**.

    Use a **dictionary** to find out the meaning of the words in **purple**.

    a) **unprecedented** ....

    1 mark

    b) **detained** ....

    1 mark

    c) **allegedly** ....

    1 mark

    d) **infamous**   ....

1 mark

    e) **vigilant**   ....

1 mark

3. Write a sentence of your own using **two**
     of the **purple** words from Question 2.

....

....

2 marks

How did you do?

Score:

LION ABOUT THE HOUSE

Vicky Maple, 33, got quiet a shock when she came
home yesterday evening to find a lion asleep on her bed.

"I was just thinking of having a nap myself, when I saw
the bed was already taken!" Maple told our reporters.

Maple called the police immediatly and was refered to
the animal department. The lion was removed safely. It is thout it
escaped from the local zoo last week. It has now been returned home.
Luckily, no-one was hurt during the adventurus lion's holiday.

"I honestly think the lion was more surprised than me," said Maple.
The zoo is yet to release a statement regarding the incident.

Number of mistakes:

Puzzle Complete? 

Spelling Practice

1. Complete the words in **bold** by
   adding the missing letters.

   All the words have endings that sound like 'shul'.

   I bought two cakes because there was a **spe**.......... offer.

   The information in the safe is strictly **confiden**.......... .

   A good judge has to be **impar**.......... .

   The reservoir isn't natural, it's **artifi**.......... .

   It is **essen**.......... to bring a map with you when hiking.

   5 marks

Vocabulary Questions

If you're not sure, use a dictionary or a thesaurus to help you.

2. Write a simpler word for each of the words in **bold** below.

   a) Freya took the **opportunity**
      to thank her friends and family.   ....

      1 mark

   b) We had a minor **dispute**, as we
      both refused to do the washing up.   ....

      1 mark

   c) The knight was known for his
      fortitude in scary situations.   ....

      1 mark

   d) There seemed to be no way
      out of our **predicament**.   ....

      1 mark

60

3. Complete these **definitions** using words from the box.

tolerance	justice	despair

.... — a feeling of great sadness

.... — when everyone is dealt with fairly

.... — the ability to put up with things
you don't like or agree with

How did you do?

3 marks

Score:

Puzzle: Find The Words

Find the missing words in the wordsearch.

D	E	S	T	I	N	Y	L	W	K
F	D	G	W	V	U	J	O	L	M
A	I	S	S	T	Y	L	Y	E	E
S	R	T	X	E	M	O	A	P	M
I	P	W	U	O	E	R	L	W	O
A	S	N	D	H	D	L	T	O	R
F	F	S	E	D	H	S	Y	I	Y
T	I	J	M	P	Z	B	F	G	R
W	G	H	O	N	E	S	T	Y	F
Q	E	H	Y	D	J	Y	K	A	N
G	O	S	S	I	P	D	O	M	S

1. The artist took p... in his work.

2. Dogs are well known for their l...

3. The teacher shared her words of w...

4. It was their d... to be together.

5. He wanted to know the latest g...

6. My earliest m... is of learning to ride a bike.

7. I hate lying — h... is important.

Puzzle Complete? 

61

Summer Term: Workout 7

Spelling Practice

1. Complete the words in **bold** by adding in the correct **silent letter**.

    The headteacher had a **solem**.......... expression during assembly.

    Sunita is **fas**..........**inated** by dinosaurs and fossils.

    The customer asked the assistant for a **recei**..........**t**.

    Dave, who is interested in cars, wants to be a **mec**..........**anic**.

    Emma panicked as she read through the **assi**..........**nment**.

    ____
    5 marks

Vocabulary Questions

2. Read the text below.

> The lorry **hurtled** down the motorway at a blistering speed. Carl had done all he could to slow the metal beast down, but the brakes had failed and he was running out of ideas. The logs he was **hauling** bounced, threatening to rip the straps which secured them. Carl smashed his fist onto the horn, creating a **deafening** noise to alert the **oblivious** drivers ahead of him.

What do you think the words in **purple** mean?
Circle the word you think is the best match.

a) **hurtled**   juddered / trundled / zoomed
____
1 mark

b) **hauling**   transporting / burning / chopping
____
1 mark

c) **deafening**   ear-splitting / voiceless / terrible

1 mark

d) **oblivious**   panicky / unaware / distinct

1 mark

3. Write down **three verbs** to do with **movement**.
    Don't use any words from Question 2 in your answer.

    ....

    ....

    ....

3 marks

How did you do?   **Score:**

Puzzle: Correct The Homework

Put yourself in your teacher's shoes. Can you spot the mistakes in this pupil's report? Circle the five misspelt words, then write down the correct spellings on the dotted lines underneath.

> Infecious diseases can be passed on from person to person. Because of this, hospitals have to be extremely caucious, and good hygiene is considered essencial. Hospitals have speshal dispensers where you can clean your hands on the go. Everyone should also be consious of their hygiene outside of the hospital, so that these diseases are kept at bay.

....

....

Puzzle Complete? ✓

Summer Term: Workout 8

Spelling Practice

1. Write the correct spelling of the words in **bold** on the lines.

    It is **possably** the worst film I've seen.   ....

    Luckily the damage wasn't **noticable**.   ....

    Priya was **visably** shaken by the news.   ....

    Mr Smith is **relyably** punctual.   ....

    We can't buy a giraffe — be **reasonible**.   ....

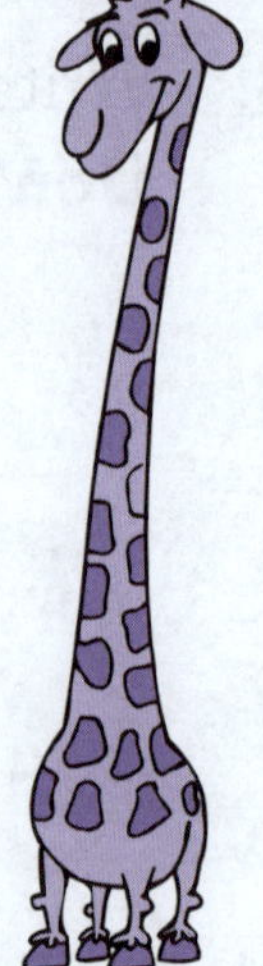

5 marks

Vocabulary Questions

2. For each pair of words in **bold**, **circle** the word
    which makes the most sense in the passage.

As Penelope reached the top floor of the

skyscraper / house, she saw the office had descended into

chaos. Some people were throwing their **briefcases / hats**

in the air, causing loose paper to rain down, while others were

throwing computers out of the window. The secretary was

hiding under his desk, desperately trying to call the boss, who

was at an important **construction / conference**. Penelope

felt **amicable / intimidated** by the complete disarray.

4 marks

64

3. What do you think the words in **purple** mean?
   Circle the word you think is the best match.

   a) **enterprise**   access / business / reward

   1 mark

   b) **salary**   wage / budget / formal

   1 mark

   c) **colleague**   sibling / team / co-worker

   1 mark

How did you do?

Score:

Puzzle: Complete The Words

Use the clues to help you complete the crossword.

Across:

3. Experiencing pain

5. A business meeting

6. A mention of something

7. Not the same

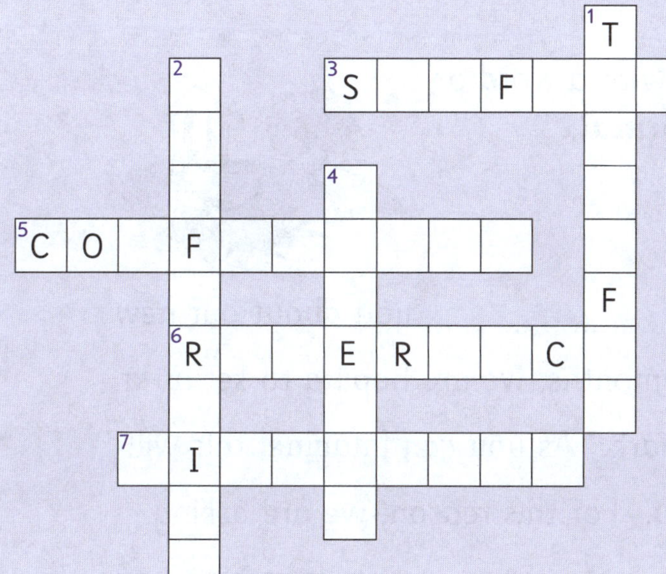

Down:

1. To move something

2. Liking something more than another thing

4. The person who ensures people obey the rules in a sports game

Puzzle Complete? 

Summer Term: Workout 8

Spelling Practice

1. **Circle** the correct spelling of the words below.

    decieve / deceive   achieve / acheive

    believe / beleive   cieling / ceiling

    percieve / perceive   concieve / conceive

    6 marks

Vocabulary Questions

2. For each sentence, **circle** the word which sounds more **formal**.

    The new play we went to see was **funny / humorous**.

    Hugh found the entire train journey **tedious / boring**.

    2 marks

3. Replace the words in **bold** with a word or
    phrase that sounds more **formal**.

    Dear Sir/Madam,

    I am writing to **tell** .... you about our new

    project. In the coming few months, we are hoping to set up a

    nature reserve next to the park. As you can imagine, this will

    take lots of time and money. For this reason, we are asking

    for your **help** .... A nature reserve

66

will have a **really good** .... impact on the
local community, as it will give families somewhere to go at the
weekend. It will also help endangered animals. I hope you will
think about .... investing in our project.

Yours faithfully,
Janet Carver

How did you do?

Score:

Puzzle: Fill The Gaps

Use the clues to complete the words.

n ☐ ☐ ☐ ☐ ☐ ☐ = *the opposite of 'everything'*

c ☐ ☐ ☐ ☐ ☐ ☐ ☐ = *made something new*

l ☐ ☐ ☐ ☐ ☐ ☐ ☐ = *a game where money is won by those with the correct ticket numbers*

m ☐ ☐ ☐ ☐ ☐ ☐ ☐ = *a combination of different substances*

b ☐ ☐ ☐ ☐ ☐ ☐ = *insects with hard shells and wings*

a ☐ ☐ ☐ ☐ ☐ = *move forward*

g ☐ ☐ ☐ ☐ ☐ ☐ = *farewell*

Unscramble the letters from the shaded
boxes to reveal the hidden word.

Hidden word: ☐ ☐ ☐ ☐ ☐ ☐ ☐

Puzzle Complete? ✓

Spelling Practice

1. Underline the words that are spelt incorrectly
    and write the correct spellings on the lines.

    Joshua felt awkwerd speaking in class.   ....

    Their neghbor owned a black labrador.   ....

    The events filled Marta with cureosity.   ....

    6 marks

Vocabulary Questions

2. For each pair of words in **bold**, **circle** the adverb
    which makes the most sense in the passage.

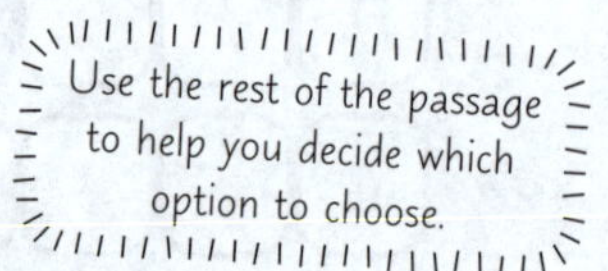

At long last, it was the day of the big race. Sasha had

been **faithfully / carelessly** training every day since her

decision to compete. As her name was called out, Sasha

made her way towards the starting line. She looked around

at her fellow competitors and realised that she was the

youngest person in the race. She **anxiously / gleefully**

glanced at her parents in the stands. They nodded

encouragingly / woefully and she felt her nerves

disappear. Sasha took a long, deep breath. "On your marks...

get set... go!" the race official shouted, and Sasha ran.

3 marks

3.   Use a **dictionary** to find out the meaning of the words.

jubilation   ....

adjudicate   ....

saunter   ....

3 marks

How did you do?   Score: [　　]

Spelling Practice

1. Complete the words in **bold** by adding a **suffix** from the box. Use each suffix once.

> ant ance ancy ent ence ency

Richard was a resid.......... at the grand old hotel.

Gabe had the dec.......... to apologise for being late.

Flora was in the last few months of her pregn.......... .

The elderly man required assist.......... to get out of bed.

Laurie was full of confid.......... before her driving test.

The angry prisoner was defi.......... and refused to co-operate.

6 marks

Vocabulary Questions

2. Choose a word from the box to complete each of the sentences. Use each word once.

> assembling shipped satisfied
> packaged develops delivery

a) An inventor .... a new product.

1 mark

b) Staff begin .... the goods in a factory.

1 mark

c) The products are .... in boxes.

1 mark

d) Then they are .... off all around the world.

1 mark

e) Local .... drivers pick up individual packages.

1 mark

f) If the customer isn't .... , they can ask for their money back.

1 mark

How did you do?

Score:

Puzzle: Palindrome Wordsearch

Find and circle six palindromes.
Use the clues to help you.

CLUE: A palindrome is a word that reads backwards the same as it reads forwards, e.g. level.

P	M	R	R	C	O	T	S	E	O
X	E	Z	F	E	G	K	K	U	R
W	V	E	F	D	F	A	F	Y	E
J	V	F	P	M	Y	E	D	A	D
C	P	K	L	A	L	X	R	I	D
E	V	V	K	M	F	J	B	Q	E
P	M	L	A	F	Q	X	P	O	R
U	V	D	Y	P	I	U	S	Q	M
K	A	D	M	Q	O	T	R	D	F
M	N	O	O	N	K	K	J	M	H

1. Similar to a canoe

2. The female equivalent of 'sir'

3. Midday

4. Have a quick look

5. More red

6. When you mention someone, you ... to them

Puzzle Complete?

Summer Term: Workout 12

Spelling Practice

1. Circle the correct words to complete the sentences below.

   Casey had to put new batteries into the **devise / device**.

   Tasha looked beautiful in her **bridle / bridal** gown.

   "**Who's / Whose** coat is this?"

   Lana couldn't find her driving **license / licence**.

   He **lead / led** the goat through the pasture.

   5 marks

Vocabulary Questions

2. Complete this short story using the words from the box.

overwhelming	dingy	excruciating	perilous

Monica's broken arm was ....
Looking up, she realised just how far she
had fallen down the mineshaft. She felt an
.... panic as she was faced with
the .... task of climbing back to
the surface. She knew she had to get out of the
.... mine as soon as possible.

4 marks

72

3. Complete the text below with **synonyms** of the words in **bold**.

Rory grimaced at the plate of broccoli as he struggled

to hide his **disdain** .... His mum knew

that the **revolting** .... stench of the

soggy, green vegetable turned his stomach, but she

was making him eat it **regardless** ....

Rory prodded at the unappetising mush with his fork.

3 marks

How did you do?

Score:

Puzzle: Word Pairs

The words on the bottom row follow the same pattern as the
words on the top. Find the missing word to complete the set.

J and A are the first and second letters in JAW

Take the same letters from the bottom words to make a new word.

JAW (**JAIL**) M**IL**K
KEYS (*KEEP*) W**EP**T

I and L are the second and third letters in MILK

a)
MASK (MAIL) SAIL
BUOY (................) LAMP

b)
TIRE (RATS) SALE
ANTS (................) REIN

c)
EARL (LASS) BOSS
LOGS (................) DECK

d)
HOST (MYTH) ARMY
KISS (................) SIDE

Puzzle Complete? ✔

Summer Term: Workout 12

Here are some tricky words — tick them off when you've learnt them.

accommodate ✓	develop ✓	necessary ✓
accompany ✓	disastrous ✓	occur ✓
according ✓	environment ✓	opportunity ✓
amateur ✓	exaggerate ✓	prejudice ✓
apparent ✓	existence ✓	privilege ✓
appreciate ✓	explanation ✓	pronunciation ✓
attached ✓	familiar ✓	recognise ✓
awkward ✓	harass ✓	relevant ✓
committee ✓	hindrance ✓	sacrifice ✓
community ✓	immediate ✓	secretary ✓
conscience ✓	immediately ✓	stomach ✓
conscious ✓	individual ✓	sufficient ✓
controversy ✓	interrupt ✓	system ✓
convenience ✓	leisure ✓	thorough ✓
correspond ✓	lightning ✓	twelfth ✓
criticise ✓	marvellous ✓	variety ✓
curiosity ✓	mischievous ✓	yacht ✓
desperate ✓		

Answers

Autumn Term

Workout 1 — pages 2-3

1. steel
   advice
   guest
   effects
   aloud
   1 mark for each correct answer

2. a) thick   1 mark   d) land   1 mark
   b) cautiously   1 mark   e) agitated   1 mark
   c) unknown   1 mark

3. There are many possible answers.
   E.g. The **unfamiliar** environment made me feel very **unsettled**.
   1 mark for each word used correctly

Puzzle: Jungle Crossword

Across:
2. HABITAT
4. RUSTLING
5. ENDANGERED

Down:
1. SWELTERING
2. HARMFUL
3. WILDER

Workout 2 — pages 4-5

1. dist**ant**
   Anci**ent**
   independ**ent**
   vali**ant**
   innoc**ent**
   1 mark for each correct answer

2. There are many possible answers.
   good — e.g. excellent, great
   bad — e.g. terrible, awful
   1 mark for each correct answer

3. There are many possible answers.
   E.g. I had a **wonderful** time this weekend. We got a train into the city and went to the aquarium. We saw so many **intriguing** sea creatures but my favourite was the shark. It was very **amusing**.
   1 mark for each correct answer

Puzzle: Water Words

wvea — **wave** — ripple
aofm — **foam** — froth
sako — **soak** — immerse
sretam — **stream** — brook

Workout 3 — pages 6-7

1. received
   deceitful
   priest
   receipt
   retrieve
   relief
   1 mark for each correct answer

2. There are many possible answers.
   inconsolable — e.g. very sad
   exasperated — e.g. annoyed
   petrified — e.g. terrified
   1 mark for each correct answer

3. a) They were so **petrified** as the monster came towards them that they screamed.   1 mark
   b) John was **exasperated** by his little brother's irritating behaviour.   1 mark
   c) Claire was **inconsolable** when she lost her necklace — she couldn't stop crying.   1 mark

Puzzle: Puzzling Emotions

1. **e**cstatic
2. **a**nxious
3. ea**g**er
4. lon**e**ly
5. te**r**rified

Your code name is **eagle**

Workout 4 — pages 8-9

1. gym
   myth
   mystery
   pyramid
   synonym
   1 mark for each correct answer

2. a) stunned   1 mark   d) scruffy   1 mark
   b) unsafely   1 mark   e) crowded   1 mark
   c) scattered   1 mark

3. There are many possible answers.
   E.g. Stacy felt **overwhelmed** as she looked at her room, which was **littered** with dirty clothes.
   1 mark for each word used correctly

Puzzle: Complete The Words

Across:
2. VAGUE
4. ANTIQUE
6. UNIQUE

Down:
1. FATIGUE
3. LEAGUE
5. TONGUE

Answers

Workout 5 — pages 10-11

1. a) vi**cious** 1 mark
    b) cau**tious** 1 mark
    c) deli**cious** 1 mark
    d) infec**tious** 1 mark
    e) suspi**cious** 1 mark
    f) nutri**tious** 1 mark

2. There are many possible answers.
    E.g. Sasha finds video games **thrilling**.
    E.g. Adrian finds exercising **challenging**.
    E.g. Pam thought the film was **hilarious**.
    1 mark for each correct answer

3. There are many possible answers.
    E.g. This morning, I had a lengthy conversation with
    a **lovely** boy who sits next to me. He said he felt
    extremely **foolish** because his mum kissed him goodbye
    in front of his friends! Then the bell rang and a teacher
    silently entered the classroom. I gulped — she looked
    incredibly **terrifying**.
    1 mark for each correct answer

Puzzle: Pyramid Puzzle

From top to bottom, the pyramid should look like this:

IN
PIN
SPIN
SPINE
PONIES
PIGEONS
EXPOSING

Workout 6 — pages 12-13

1. special
    essential
    social
    confidential
    potential
    1 mark for each correct answer

2. There are many possible answers.
    E.g. The nurse soothed the **anxious** patient.
    E.g. The ambulance **raced** past other
    cars, its lights flashing brightly.
    E.g. The doctor **allowed** the unwell
    woman to go for a walk.
    1 mark for each correct answer

3. Dear Mr Mahmood,
    I am writing to **confirm** your **appointment** on
    Thursday 15th May at 09:15. Please arrive at the
    hospital at least 10 minutes beforehand, as we will
    require you to fill out a short **questionnaire** before
    seeing the doctor.
    1 mark for each correct answer

Puzzle: Missing Link
SPACE **SHIP** WRECK
CAMP **FIRE** MAN
FOOT **BALL** ROOM
POP **CORN** FLAKE
FAMILY **TREE** HOUSE

The shaded boxes spell **PEACE**.

Workout 7 — pages 14-15

1. ador**ation**
    divi**sion**
    discu**ssion**
    politi**cian**
    fic**tion**
    1 mark for each correct answer

2. a) valley   1 mark   c) reaches   1 mark
    b) continually   1 mark   d) destroy   1 mark

3. There are many possible answers.
    flowing — e.g. cascading
    landscape — e.g. terrain
    changing — e.g. transforming
    1 mark for each correct answer

Puzzle: Rock Crossword

Across: Down:
3. MOUNTAIN   1. BOULDER
4. CLIFF   2. PEBBLE
5. CLIMBER

Workout 8 — pages 16-17

1. toler**ance**
    vac**ancy**
    emerg**ency**
    evid**ence**
    arrog**ance**
    1 mark for each correct answer

2. a) "It's your fault we lost it!" **snapped** Jess.   1 mark
    b) "Perhaps we could look in the shed?" **suggested**
       Mark.   1 mark
    c) "I have a secret," **confided** Olivia.   1 mark

3. There are many possible answers.
    E.g. "Where were you the night the amulets were stolen
    from the museum?" **asked** the inspector.
    "I was out with work colleagues. You can check with
    them," **replied** Alastair.
    "That's funny," **sneered** the inspector, "because we have
    evidence to the contrary."
    "Impossible!" **snarled** Alastair, with a menacing gleam
    in his eyes.
    1 mark for each correct answer

Puzzle: Correct The Homework

The incorrect words are:
concieted (conceited), perseved (perceived),
inconseivable (inconceivable), recieve (receive)

Workout 9 — pages 18-19

1. caffeine
   anxious
   initial
   assistance
   provincial
   1 mark for each correct answer

2. There are many possible answers.
   First picture — e.g. haunted, eerie
   Second picture — e.g. peaceful, remote
   1 mark for each correct answer

3. There are many possible answers.
   E.g. It was **tranquil** in the mountains.
   E.g. The prison cell was **dreary**.
   E.g. London is very **hectic** today.
   1 mark for each correct answer

Puzzle: Word Pyramids

From top to bottom, the first
pyramid should look like this:

OR   OUR   HOUR   ROUGH

From top to bottom, the second
pyramid should look like this:

TEN   TEND   TREND   TENDER

Workout 10 — pages 20-21

1. improve
   busy
   water
   hours
   beautiful
   clothes
   1 mark for each correct answer

2. There are many possible answers.
   exhilarated — e.g. very happy
   preoccupied — e.g. distracted
   despondent — e.g. very unhappy
   1 mark for each correct answer

3. The artist was very quiet — she wasn't unhappy, just
   preoccupied.
   Lena felt **exhilarated** after receiving thunderous
   applause.
   His defeat had left him completely **despondent**.
   1 mark for each correct answer

Puzzle: Corrections Crossword

Across:
5. AGAIN
6. EVERYBODY

Down:
1. BECAUSE
2. SUGAR
3. CLIMB
4. ONLY

Workout 11 — pages 22-23

1. forgotten
   gardening
   referee
   beginners'
   preferred
   1 mark for each correct answer

2. rich — destitute
   immaculate — scruffy
   conscientious — careless
   2 marks for 2 or 3 correct, otherwise
   1 mark for 1 correct

3. There are many possible answers
   a) E.g. Hedgehogs are **rare** in this area.   1 mark
   b) E.g. The books in the library were **modern**.   1 mark
   c) E.g. The sea was very **rough** when we were on the
      cruise.   1 mark
   d) E.g. The exchange student was **rude** to the host
      family.   1 mark
   e) E.g. We had **adequate** supplies to get us through the
      long journey.   1 mark

Puzzle: Antonym Wordsearch

The words are:

deep — shallow
safe — dangerous
positive — negative
create — destroy
blunt — sharp
lowest — highest
ancient — modern

A	E	D	E	S	T	R	O	Y	A	S
S	H	A	R	P	X	B	U	P	D	M
O	E	N	W	S	V	H	J	K	P	O
A	S	G	G	H	N	M	R	E	F	D
S	N	E	G	A	T	I	V	E	K	E
P	F	R	I	L	D	X	O	U	E	R
Y	D	O	H	L	J	E	R	O	G	N
J	D	U	U	O	K	F	M	L	H	U
D	U	S	I	W	R	H	E	N	W	V
W	R	H	I	G	H	E	S	T	F	I

Workout 12 — pages 24-25

1. considerably
   changeable
   edible
   adorable
   terribly
   1 mark for each correct answer

2. Addition words — moreover, furthermore
   Contrast words — conversely, however
   1 mark for each correct answer

Answers

3. Learning another language can help you find out information while you're on holiday. **Furthermore / Moreover**, it gives you the chance to befriend people you wouldn't normally speak to. **Moreover / Furthermore**, it can be fun to learn a language. **However / Conversely**, many people don't find it fun because learning a language can be difficult.
1 mark for each correct answer

Puzzle: Word Wheel

Some words you could have found are: be, bet, let, tie, abet, able, bale, beat, belt, bite, blue, late, leaf, tile, tube, fable, table, beautiful

The nine-letter word is: beautiful

Spring Term

Workout 1 — pages 26-27

1. **dis**appear
   unfamiliar
   incorrect
   impossible
   misbehave
   1 mark for each correct answer

2. a) E.g. book   1 mark
   b) E.g. discovered   1 mark

3. There are many possible answers.
   looking — e.g. peering
   interesting — e.g. captivating
   searching — e.g. exploring
   things — e.g. artefacts
   said — e.g. cried
   1 mark for each correct answer

Puzzle: Ancient Crossword

Across:
4. TOMB
6. FOSSIL
7. STATUE

Down:
1. PAST
2. CASTLE
3. RUINS
5. MUSEUM

Workout 2 — pages 28-29

1. Alan wanted to interrupt and tell her not to <u>exagerate</u>. — exaggerate
   Taking the aggressive rhino on the boat was a <u>disatrus</u> idea. — disastrous
   Erin started a <u>comittee</u> to work on saving the environment. — committee
   1 mark for each correctly underlined answer and 1 mark for each correct spelling

2. There are many possible answers.
   dilapidated — e.g. rickety
   malevolent — e.g. malicious
   ghastly — e.g. horrific
   1 mark for each correct answer

3. As I stumbled through the dark forest, I could sense a **malevolent** presence watching me. Eventually, I came to a **dilapidated** cabin. I was about to enter when I heard a **ghastly** scream.
   1 mark for each correct answer

Puzzle: Scary Words

cerepy — **creepy** — eerie
treorr — **terror** — dread
eivl — **evil** — malicious
anabndoed — **abandoned** — deserted

Workout 3 — pages 30-31

1. **k**nowledge
   balle**t**
   fastened
   plum**b**er
   i**s**land
   1 mark for each correct answer

2. Today we paid a visit to the zoo. I was terrified of the lion because it looked **vicious**. The crocodile also had **razor-sharp** teeth. The giraffe seemed very **docile** as it quietly ate some leaves. At midday, we saw a penguin parade **waddling** through the zoo. We then visited the meerkats, which stared at us **inquisitively** as if we were the zoo animals, not them.
   1 mark for each correct answer

3. There are many possible answers.
   E.g. Jonah and Gill set off for the animal shelter with their parents. When they arrived, a puppy **bounded** over to them and licked their faces. He seemed like a very **lively** dog indeed.
   1 mark for each correct answer

Puzzle: Animal Wordsearch

The words are:
1. hibernate
2. docile
3. soared
4. adapted
5. pranced
6. howled
7. carnivore

A	G	Y	H	U	G	B	S	E	J	I
D	F	J	U	O	I	O	P	Z	E	H
E	F	J	K	O	W	F	G	T	C	I
O	U	V	G	U	K	L	M	K	A	B
W	S	O	A	R	E	D	E	A	R	E
S	D	F	J	U	E	C	X	D	N	R
Z	V	D	O	C	I	L	E	A	I	N
D	S	W	N	B	N	Y	K	L	V	A
S	E	A	I	U	N	I	N	G	O	T
E	R	F	G	J	I	N	N	E	R	E
P	Q	F	H	A	D	A	P	T	E	D

Workout 4 — pages 32-33

1. spitefully
   arrogantly
   venomously
   maliciously
   courageously
   1 mark for each correct answer

2. There are many possible answers.
E.g. Cara was awarded the medal for acting **bravely** in the face of danger.
E.g. Mario had hurt his back, so he sat down very **carefully**.
E.g. Shanice looked up **nervously** when she heard her name being shouted.
1 mark for each correct answer

3. Marcus gave **generously** to charity.
Mo shook the bottle **vigorously** until it exploded.
Tim was **gradually** becoming more confident with his driving.
Alice had **ingeniously** invented a device which would tidy her room for her.
1 mark for each correct answer

Puzzle: Detective's Assistant

The robbery happened at **night**. According to our **source(s)** of information, the thief stole £1000. Witnesses reported seeing a **stationary** white van waiting outside the bank. It is believed the thief has fled abroad, possibly to the **desert**.

Workout 5 — pages 34-35

1. altar
draught
alter
affect
draft
effect
1 mark for each correct answer

2. a) prophesy   1 mark
b) patrol   1 mark
c) complement   1 mark
d) attribute   1 mark
e) contract   1 mark
f) permit   1 mark

Puzzle: Personality Wordsearch

1. Word: **modest**   Synonym: e.g. **humble**
2. Word: **caring**   Synonym: e.g. **loving**
3. Word: **reliable**   Synonym: e.g. **dependable**
4. Word: **creative**   Synonym: e.g. **artistic**
5. Word: **nasty**   Synonym: e.g. **unpleasant**

W	Y	U	S	D	E	N	C	E	J	F
P	Q	D	B	F	U	L	R	R	L	G
R	E	L	I	A	B	L	E	H	E	B
J	M	O	D	E	S	T	A	Y	U	N
X	V	K	H	Y	S	R	T	I	S	J
F	N	G	B	N	U	O	I	N	J	K
C	A	R	I	N	G	F	V	G	O	L
T	S	V	P	U	F	K	E	F	L	I
S	T	R	E	H	U	Y	K	D	I	O
X	Y	K	T	E	M	G	N	K	S	W
C	V	G	T	N	G	Y	I	U	W	S

Workout 6 — pages 36-37

1. co-operate
co-own
re-evaluate
re-enter
pre-arrange
pre-order
1 mark for each correct answer

2. a) unwell   1 mark
b) brilliant   1 mark
c) thrilled   1 mark
d) a lot of money   1 mark
e) raining heavily   1 mark
f) was exactly right   1 mark

Puzzle: Mixed Messages

1. dominated
2. opposition
3. superbly
4. brilliance
5. superior

Do you think they won? **Yes**

Workout 7 — pages 38-39

1. He had to flee the <u>contry</u> immediately. — **country**
Lena finished the dance with a <u>florish</u>. — **flourish**
The ocean was extremely <u>rugh</u> that day. — **rough**
1 mark for each correctly underlined answer and 1 mark for each correct spelling

2. a) climbed 1 mark
b) wandered 1 mark
c) dashing 1 mark
d) echoed 1 mark

3. There are many possible answers.
E.g. We meandered across a field then clambered up a small hill.
1 mark for each word used correctly

Puzzle: Adventure Verbs Wordsearch

The words are:
1. struggled
2. traipsed
3. intensify
4. scrambled
5. wrestled
6. sneaked

R	T	C	D	R	J	U	I	A	U	S
W	R	E	S	T	L	E	D	F	G	T
E	A	Y	T	J	I	P	Z	M	V	R
Q	I	N	T	E	N	S	I	F	Y	U
S	P	F	G	H	U	J	V	E	R	G
P	S	N	E	A	K	E	D	O	R	G
C	E	G	H	Y	J	U	O	W	E	L
S	D	E	G	H	B	V	I	Y	N	E
S	C	R	A	M	B	L	E	D	E	D

Workout 8 — pages 40-41

1. All three girls' pencils needed sharpening immediately.
The children's favourite game was noughts and crosses.
1 mark for each correct answer

2. Four vans' engines were abandoned in the yard.
The teachers were getting ready for parents' evening.
Witches' spells are usually written in rhyme.
1 mark for each correct answer

Answers

3. There are many possible answers.
advantageous — e.g. helpful or useful
prestigious — e.g. having a good reputation
exceptional — e.g. very good
thrilling — e.g. very exciting
1 mark for each correct answer

4. The new supermarket will be **advantageous** to all of us.
The dancers put on an **exceptional** performance.
The actress received the most **prestigious** award at the ceremony.
1 mark for each correct answer

Puzzle: Unscramble And Search

The words are:
1. descend
2. science
3. fascinated
4. muscle
5. ascend
6. scenery

Y	U	D	E	G	H	U	I	N	B
M	T	E	D	V	I	B	N	R	Z
J	U	K	Q	R	D	E	I	K	C
I	N	S	S	F	G	L	L	D	O
F	A	S	C	I	N	A	T	E	D
R	K	J	I	L	M	E	J	S	N
I	Q	C	E	Z	E	M	R	C	E
C	E	P	N	I	W	G	K	E	C
N	G	M	C	G	K	X	I	N	S
R	S	C	E	N	E	R	Y	D	A

Workout 9 — pages 42-43

1. tougher
naughty
bough
fought
burrow
1 mark for each correct answer

2. There are many possible answers.
disgusting — e.g. revolting
deadly — e.g. lethal
subterranean — e.g. underground
1 mark for each correct answer

3. There are many possible answers.
E.g. The snake hissed, showing its **deadly** fangs.
1 mark for any sensible answer

4. There are many possible answers.
E.g. stuck, worried, winged
1 mark for each correct answer

Puzzle: Creepy-Crawly Crossword

Across:
1. SPIDER
4. MICROSCOPE
5. HABITAT
7. NOCTURNAL

Down:
2. POISONOUS
3. PREDATOR
6. SLIMY

Workout 10 — pages 44-45

1. cemetery
environment
yacht
secretary
lightning
familiar
1 mark for each correct answer

2. There are many possible answers.
abundant — e.g. plentiful
pristine — e.g. in good condition
temperate — e.g. not too hot or too cold
1 mark for each correct answer

3. The forest was in a **temperate** climate.
The snow was **pristine** because we were the first people to walk on it.
Wildflowers were **abundant** on the tropical island.
1 mark for each correct answer

Puzzle: Nature Wordsearch

The words are:
1. lush
2. foliage
3. fertile
4. evergreen
5. glacier
6. peaceful
7. wilderness

E	V	E	R	G	R	E	E	N	W
T	Y	S	F	L	V	S	O	P	I
C	T	E	G	A	F	E	D	N	L
X	A	Q	L	C	L	N	U	P	D
W	F	O	L	I	A	G	E	I	E
S	F	B	T	E	M	K	L	O	R
K	B	R	E	R	A	D	F	H	N
A	E	F	G	Y	J	O	E	R	E
F	Z	E	N	H	L	U	S	H	S
P	E	A	C	E	F	U	L	R	S
S	F	I	O	F	G	Y	A	D	C

Workout 11 — pages 46-47

1. mission
coronation
politician
animation
magician
tension
1 mark for each correct answer

2. We had picked the perfect place to camp. The birds were **chattering** and we could hear the gentle **trickle** of the stream nearby. The fire was **crackling** away as we warmed our hands by it. We were just about to put up the tents when we heard the distant **rumble** of thunder.
1 mark for each correct answer

3. There are many possible answers.
    bellow — e.g. shout
    screech — e.g. scream
    1 mark for each correct answer

Puzzle: Complete The Words

<u>Across:</u>
1. ACHIEVE
6. PARLIAMENT
7. RHYME

<u>Down:</u>
2. VARIETY
3. QUEUE
4. BRUISE
5. OCCUR

Workout 12 — pages 48-49

1. adven**ture**
    enclo**sure**
    crea**ture**
    trea**sure**
    pic**ture**
    1 mark for each correct answer

2. a) determined   1 mark   c) flamboyant   1 mark
    b) arrogant   1 mark   d) humble   1 mark

3. There are many possible answers.
    shrewd — e.g. having good judgement
    innovative — e.g. using new ideas
    candid — e.g. honest
    1 mark for each correct answer

Puzzle: Find The Criminal

This man is wanted for trying to take over the world. He has a thin **moustache** and wears a **flamboyant** hat. If you see a **mysterious** character wearing a cape, please report him to the police. He is known to be very **devious**.

Summer Term

Workout 1 — pages 50-51

1. mountainous
    courageous
    glamorous
    famous
    furious
    1 mark for each correct answer

2. Tired of the British rain? Why not make the peaceful, **exotic** shores of the Caribbean your next holiday **destination**? Stay on a distant island at our new spa retreat. Enjoy the **solitude** of the quiet beaches, or go on a trip to the **bustling** markets of the nearby town. Make the most of our luxurious swimming pool and spa facilities for no extra cost.
    1 mark for each correct answer

3. There are many possible answers.
    distant — e.g. far-off
    trip — e.g. excursion
    luxurious — e.g. lavish
    1 mark for each correct answer

Puzzle: Holiday Pyramids

From top to bottom, the first pyramid should look like this:

NO   ONE   CONE   OCEAN

From top to bottom, the second pyramid should look like this:

FIG   GIFT   FIGHT   FLIGHT

Workout 2 — pages 52-53

1. cough
    fort
    ought
    thorough
    scoff
    1 mark for each correct answer

2. a) grateful   1 mark   c) punctual   1 mark
    b) food   1 mark   d) tiredness   1 mark

3. Dear student,
    The school is hosting an event to welcome our French exchange students. The event will begin at 4:30 pm. Traditional French **cuisine** will be served, as well as a selection of classic English snacks. We would be **appreciative** if you could be **prompt** so we can begin on time.
    1 mark for each correct answer

Puzzle: Missing Link

TEXT **BOOK** SHELF
TRAP **DOOR** BELL
WORK **SHOP** LIFT
HORSE **SHOE** LACE
BED **ROOM** MATE

The hidden word is: **BROOM**

Workout 3 — pages 54-55

1. scheming
    chalet
    chemist
    parachute
    chorus
    1 mark for each correct answer

2. Mr Hempton was relieved that the chaotic school trip was over. To begin with, Marion had **absentmindedly** stepped in front of a bus, causing the bus driver to screech to a halt to avoid hitting the careless student. Next, Douglas had **recklessly** run off. Luckily, Ms Simms managed to find him and marched him back to the group, looking at him **reproachfully**. All of this made them late, so they had to walk **briskly** to the museum.
    1 mark for each correct answer

Answers

3. There are many possible answers.
E.g. Rachel smiled **fondly** at the old photo.
E.g. Bryan worked **diligently** for the exam.
E.g. The film was **genuinely** based on a true story.
1 mark for each correct answer

Puzzle: Adverbs Wordsearch

The words are:
1. frantically
2. moderately
3. finally
4. greedily
5. tolerably
6. gracefully

F	R	A	N	T	I	C	A	L	L	Y
S	D	E	R	O	T	Y	U	I	N	G
Y	U	O	P	L	X	V	G	J	R	R
W	E	J	Y	E	V	R	I	E	O	F
M	O	D	E	R	A	T	E	L	Y	I
X	C	H	U	A	K	D	R	U	I	N
Z	X	G	J	B	I	R	Y	I	O	A
S	D	Y	U	L	J	E	I	N	K	L
A	V	G	Y	Y	P	O	Y	V	A	L
O	R	D	G	A	F	I	E	R	L	Y
G	R	A	C	E	F	U	L	L	Y	S

Workout 4 — pages 56-57

1. precious
infectious
ambitious
spacious
fictitious
1 mark for each correct answer

2. increase — go up
decrease — go down
estimate — guess
deduce — figure out
3 marks for 3 or 4 correct, 2 marks for
2 correct, 1 mark for 1 correct

3. There are many possible answers.
E.g. It is really difficult for scientists to tell when a
volcano is going to erupt. They often **observe** the
volcano to see if its appearance has changed. You can
also **discover** a lot about a volcano from the number
of earthquakes that happen nearby. If the number of
earthquakes **increases**, this sometimes means that the
volcano might erupt soon. Scientists **attempt** to give
people as much warning as possible.
1 mark for each correct answer

Puzzle: Complete The Words

Across:
3. EIGHT
4. VEIL
6. NEIGHBOUR
7. OBEY

Down:
1. WEIGHT
2. VEINS
5. PREY

Workout 5 — pages 58-59

1. co-ordinate
re-enter
co-operate
co-own
re-evaluate
1 mark for each correct answer

2. There are many possible answers.
a) unprecedented — e.g. has never
happened before   1 mark
b) detained — e.g. arrested   1 mark
c) allegedly — e.g. supposedly   1 mark
d) infamous — e.g. known for having
a bad reputation   1 mark
e) vigilant — e.g. paying attention to danger   1 mark

3. There are many possible answers.
E.g. We decided to be vigilant after the unprecedented
increase in car thefts.
1 mark for each word used correctly

Puzzle: Newspaper Editor

The incorrect words are:
quiet (quite), immediatly (immediately), refered (referred)
thout (thought), adventurus (adventurous)

There are **5** mistakes.

Workout 6 — pages 60-61

1. spe**cial**
confiden**tial**
impar**tial**
artifi**cial**
essen**tial**
1 mark for each correct answer

2. There are many possible answers.
a) E.g. Freya took the **chance** to thank her friends and
family.   1 mark
b) E.g. We had a minor **argument**, as we both refused
to do the washing up.   1 mark
c) E.g. The knight was known for his **bravery** in scary
situations.   1 mark
d) E.g. There seemed to be no way out of our **situation**.
1 mark

3. **despair** — a feeling of great sadness
justice — when everyone is dealt with fairly
tolerance — the ability to put up with things you don't
like or agree with
1 mark for each correct answer

Answers

82

Puzzle: Find The Words

The words are:
1. pride   5. gossip
2. loyalty   6. memory
3. wisdom   7. honesty
4. destiny

D	E	S	T	I	N	Y	L	W	K	D
F	D	G	W	V	U	J	O	L	M	E
A	I	S	S	T	Y	L	Y	E	E	S
S	R	T	X	E	M	O	A	P	M	X
I	P	W	U	O	E	R	L	O	O	U
A	S	N	D	H	D	L	T	O	R	I
F	F	S	E	D	H	S	Y	I	Y	I
T	I	J	M	P	Z	B	F	G	R	N
W	G	H	O	N	E	S	T	Y	F	G
Q	E	H	Y	D	J	Y	K	A	N	Y
G	O	S	S	I	P	D	O	M	S	D

Workout 7 — pages 62-63

1. sole**n**
    fas**c**inated
    recei**pt**
    mec**h**anic
    assi**g**nment
    1 mark for each correct answer

2. a) zoomed   *1 mark*   c) ear-splitting   *1 mark*
    b) transporting   *1 mark*   d) unaware   *1 mark*

3. There are many possible answers.
    E.g. bounce, leapt, hike
    1 mark for each correct answer

Puzzle: Correct The Homework

The incorrect words are:
infecious (infectious), caucious (cautious), essencial (essential),
speshal (special), consious (conscious)

Workout 8 — pages 64-65

1. possibly
    noticeable
    visibly
    reliably
    reasonable
    1 mark for each correct answer

2. As Penelope reached the top floor of the **skyscraper**,
    she saw the office had descended into chaos. Some
    people were throwing their **briefcases** in the air, causing
    loose paper to rain down, while others were throwing
    computers out of the window. The secretary was hiding
    under his desk, desperately trying to call the boss,
    who was at an important **conference**. Penelope felt
    intimidated by the complete disarray.
    1 mark for each correct answer

3. a) business   *1 mark*   c) co-worker   *1 mark*
    b) wage   *1 mark*

Puzzle: Complete The Words

Across:
3. SUFFERING
5. CONFERENCE
6. REFERENCE
7. DIFFERENT

Down:
1. TRANSFER
2. PREFERRING
4. REFEREE

Workout 9 — pages 66-67

1. deceive
    believe
    perceive
    achieve
    ceiling
    conceive
    1 mark for each correct answer

2. The new play we went to see was **humorous**.
    Hugh found the entire train journey **tedious**.
    1 mark for each correct answer

3. There are many possible answers.
    E.g. Dear Sir/Madam,
    I am writing to **inform** you about our new project. In
    the coming few months, we are hoping to set up a
    nature reserve next to the park. As you can imagine,
    this will take lots of time and money. For this reason,
    we are asking for your **assistance**. A nature reserve
    will have a **positive** impact on the local community, as
    it will give families somewhere to go at the weekend.
    It will also help endangered animals. I hope you will
    consider investing in our project.
    Yours faithfully,
    Janet Carver
    1 mark for each correct answer

Puzzle: Fill The Gaps

not**h**ing
creat**e**d
lott**er**y
mi**x**ture
b**ee**tles
ad**v**ance
good**b**ye

The letters **h e e i e v b** can
be rearranged to make **beehive**.

Workout 10 — pages 68-69

1. Joshua felt <u>awkwerd</u> speaking in class. — **awkward**
    Their <u>neghbor</u> owned a black labrador. — **neighbour**
    The events filled Marta with <u>cureosity</u>. — **curiosity**
    1 mark for each correct answer

83

Answers

2. At long last, it was the day of the big race. Sasha had been **faithfully** training every day since her decision to compete. As her name was called out, Sasha made her way towards the starting line. She looked around at her fellow competitors and realised that she was the youngest person in the race. She **anxiously** glanced at her parents in the stands. They nodded **encouragingly** and she felt her nerves disappear. Sasha took a long, deep breath. "On your marks... get set... go!" the race official shouted, and Sasha ran.
    1 mark for each correct answer

3. There are many possible answers.
    jubilation — e.g. happiness
    adjudicate — e.g. judge
    saunter — e.g. walk slowly
    1 mark for each correct answer

Puzzle: Secret Message

The incorrect words are:
thur (the), brige (bridge), tresure (treasure), Yule (You'll), fined (find), undur (under), sum (some)

Hidden message: You'll find some treasure under the bridge.

Workout 11 — pages 70-71

1. resid**ent**
    dec**ency**
    pregn**ancy**
    assist**ance**
    confid**ence**
    defi**ant**
    1 mark for each correct answer

2. a) An inventor **develops** a new product.   1 mark
    b) Staff begin **assembling** the goods in a factory.
       1 mark
    c) The products are **packaged** in boxes.   1 mark
    d) Then they are **shipped** off all around the world.
       1 mark
    e) Local **delivery** drivers pick up individual packages.
       1 mark
    f) If the customer isn't **satisfied**, they can ask for their
       money back.   1 mark

Puzzle: Palindrome Wordsearch

The words are:
1. kayak   4. peep
2. madam   5. redder
3. noon   6. refer

P	M	R	R	C	O	T	S	E	O
X	E	Z	F	E	G	K	K	U	R
W	V	E	F	D	F	A	F	Y	E
J	V	F	P	M	Y	E	D	A	D
C	P	K	L	A	L	X	R	I	D
E	V	V	K	M	F	J	B	Q	E
P	M	L	A	F	Q	X	P	O	R
U	V	D	Y	P	I	U	S	Q	M
K	A	D	M	Q	O	T	R	D	F
M	N	O	O	N	K	K	J	M	H

Workout 12 — pages 72-73

1. device
    bridal
    Whose
    licence
    led
    1 mark for each correct answer

2. Monica's broken arm was **excruciating**. Looking up, she realised just how far she had fallen down the mineshaft. She felt an **overwhelming** panic as she was faced with the **perilous** task of climbing back to the surface. She knew she had to get out of the **dingy** mine as soon as possible.
    1 mark for each correct answer

3. There are many possible answers.
    E.g. Rory grimaced at the plate of broccoli as he struggled to hide his **disgust**.
    His mum knew that the **foul** stench of the soggy, green vegetable turned his stomach, but she was making him eat it **anyway**. Rory prodded at the unappetising mush with his fork.
    1 mark for each correct answer

Puzzle: Word Pairs

a) BUMP   c) SOCK
b) TEAR   d) DESK

Answers